D1123484

# BATWOMAN

## VOLUME 1 HYDROLOGY

# BATWOMAN

## VOLUME 1 HYDROLOGY

J.H. **WILLIAMS III**  W. HADEN **BLACKMAN** writers

J.H. **WILLIAMS III** artist

AMY **REEDER** & RICHARD **FRIEND**
artists – "Beyond a Shadow," Kate sequence

DAVE **STEWART** colorist

TODD **KLEIN** letterer

J.H. **WILLIAMS III** collection & series cover artist

**BATMAN** created by BOB **KANE**

MIKE MARTS Editor – Original Series  HARVEY RICHARDS  JANELLE ASSELIN Associate Editors – Original Series
RICKEY PURDIN Assistant Editor– Original Series  PETER HAMBOUSSI Editor
ROBBIN BROSTERMAN Design Director – Books  ROBBIE BIEDERMAN Publication Design

EDDIE BERGANZA Executive Editor
BOB HARRAS VP – Editor-in-Chief

DIANE NELSON President  DAN DIDIO and JIM LEE Co-Publishers
GEOFF JOHNS Chief Creative Officer
JOHN ROOD Executive VP – Sales, Marketing and Business Development
AMY GENKINS Senior VP – Business and Legal Affairs  NAIRI GARDINER Senior VP – Finance
JEFF BOISON VP – Publishing Operations  MARK CHIARELLO VP – Art Direction and Design
JOHN CUNNINGHAM VP – Marketing  TERRI CUNNINGHAM VP – Talent Relations and Services
ALISON GILL Senior VP – Manufacturing and Operations  DAVID HYDE VP – Publicity
HANK KANALZ Senior VP – Digital  JAY KOGAN VP – Business and Legal Affairs, Publishing
JACK MAHAN VP – Business Affairs, Talent  NICK NAPOLITANO VP – Manufacturing Administration
SUE POHJA VP – Book Sales  COURTNEY SIMMONS Senior VP – Publicity
BOB WAYNE Senior VP – Sales

BATWOMAN VOLUME ONE: HYDROLOGY

DC Comics, 1700 Broadway, New York, NY 10019
A Warner Bros. Entertainment Company.
Printed by RR Donnelley, Salem, VA, USA. 5/11/12. First Printing.

HC ISBN: 978-1-4012-3465-2
SC ISBN: 978-1-4012-3784-4

Certified Chain of Custody
At Least 25% Certified Forest Content
www.sfiprogram.org
SFI-01042
APPLIES TO TEXT STOCK ONLY

SUSTAINABLE
FORESTRY
INITIATIVE

Library of Congress Cataloging-in-Publication Data

Williams, J. H., III.
Batwoman volume one : hydrology / J.H. Williams III, W. Haden Blackman.
p. cm.
"Originally published in single magazine form in Batwoman 0-5"—T.p. verso.
ISBN 978-1-4012-3465-2
1. Graphic novels.  I. Blackman, W. Haden. II. Title. III. Title: Hydrology.
PN6728.B365W55 2012
741.5'973—dc23
2012002252

# BEYOND A

J.H. WILLIAMS III:
writer - artist

W. HADEN BLACKMAN:
co-writer

AMY REEDER:
artist - Kate sequence

RICHARD FRIEND:
inker - Kate sequence

SHADOW

DAVE STEWART: colorist  TODD KLEIN: letterer  JANELLE SIEGEL: associate editor  MIKE MARTS: editor  Batman created by BOB KANE

The move she uses doesn't exist in any fighting styles I've studied. It's something she invented herself. Almost got the best of me.

It's not just the move that gives her away...

...it's the way her eyes burn.

Those eyes tell me she won't ever be a victim again.

I'm not sure what she's after...

...but this is far from over.

Batwoman assessment. Final conclusion.

Regarding her civilian identity, my theory proved correct.

Kate Kane is Batwoman.

Her training is excellent and she has all the right instincts.

More important, she has the one thing I can't teach. That hole inside her that can't ever be filled, no matter how many criminals she takes down...it gives her the drive to do this.

It's time she and I have a serious discussion about the future.

I'LL CONTACT YOU AS SOON AS I KNOW *ANYTHING.*

THANK YOU FOR YOUR HELP, DETECTIVE SAWYER.

KATE? KATE *KANE?*

WHAT ARE *YOU* DOING HERE?

I CAME TO SEE YOU. AND THEN...

THAT'S RENEE...RENEE MONTOYA.

YEAH, I KNOW.

IT'S EITHER A STROKE OF BRILLIANCE...

INFILTRATION

Katie Kubert: asst. ed.

Janelle Asselin: assoc. ed.

Michael Marts: editor

Batman created by Bob Kane

WHAT THE HELL IS THIS...?

HEY! THIS AREA IS *OFF-LIMITS* TO MOTOR VEHICLES!

THIS SAYS I CAN PRETTY MUCH PARK WHEREVER I *WANT*, DETECTIVE SAWYER.

GCPD

OKAY... WHY IS THE D.E.O. IN GOTHAM?

I DIDN'T THINK YOU WERE TASKED WITH CHASING DOWN CHILD MURDERERS.

NO. THAT'S YOUR PROBLEM FOR NOW.

WE WANT *BATWOMAN*.

--PICK MY BEER-GOGGLE GIRL BEFORE I HAVE ANOTHER--

--NOT LEAVING WITH THE SAME PERSON I CAME WITH--

UGH.

JESUS CHRIST, THE DAY I'VE HAD, YOU WOULDN'T *BELIEVE* IT.

IS THIS WHERE I CALL YOU "HONEY"?

YEAH. GO ON, YOU'RE DOING GREAT. LIKE WE'RE AN OLD MARRIED COUPLE ALREADY.

OKAY, SO ON TOP OF DEALING WITH THIS WHOLE WEEPING WOMAN CASE, AND GORDON CRAWLING UP MY ASS--

*NOT* A VISUAL I NEEDED...

--NOW I HAVE SOME GOVERNMENT *BUREAUCRAT* SHADOWING ME.

WHY YOU?

THE BOAT-
HOUSE...IT STARTED
AT THE **BOATHOUSE**,
DIDN'T IT?

YOU'RE
COMMITTING A
**FELONY!**

STOP!!

THERE
YOU ARE...

AGENT
CHASE?

I KNOW
WHERE YOU CAN FIND
BATWOMAN...

Rickey Purdin: assistant editor

Harvey Richards: associate editor
Michael Marts: editor

OKAY! OKAY! I'M COMING.

HELLO, KATE'S PHONE.

UH...

HI, IS *KATE* THERE? KATE KANE?

NO. SHE'S OUT.

YOU SURE?

UH, YEAH. NOT MANY PLACES TO *HIDE* HERE.

YOU GONNA LEAVE A *MESSAGE*, OR...

YEAH, OKAY...NO. I'LL TRACK HER DOWN.

OOH, DRAMA'S COMING...

BETTE... IT'S OVER.

THIS POOL IS FOR ENLISTED ONLY, MA'AM.

MY *VICODIN* IS STARTING TO WEAR OFF, COLONEL, SO I DON'T HAVE TIME FOR YOU TO BE *CUTE* WITH ME.

JUST ANSWER MY DAMN *QUESTIONS.*

*SIR.*

WITH ALL DUE RESPECT, MA'AM, UNLESS YOU HAVE A *GENERAL* WITH YOU, I CANNOT BE COMPELLED TO TELL YOU ANYTHING.

YOU WERE KID-NAPPED A FEW MONTHS AGO BY A TERRORIST, *CORRECT?* AND *RESCUED* BY THE BATWOMAN?

I CAN'T ANSWER THAT, MA'AM, ON THE GROUNDS THAT IT MIGHT COMPROMISE NATIONAL SECURITY.

THEN TELL ME THIS...

ARE YOU PROUD OF YOUR *DAUGHTER,* SIR?

EXCUSE ME?

SHE TRIED TO FOLLOW IN YOUR FOOTSTEPS BUT WAS *DRUMMED OUT* OF WEST POINT, RIGHT?

AND FROM WHAT I *HEAR,* SHE PARTIES ALL NIGHT, THEN SLEEPS ALL DAY IN A PENTHOUSE BUILT WITH YOUR *WIFE'S MONEY.*

NO, I GUESS NOT. NOT RIGHT *NOW.* NOT UNTIL SHE STARTS DOING SOMETHING WORTHWHILE WITH HER LIFE.

WE'RE *DONE* HERE, MA'AM.

BUT I WONDER, IF *YOUR* FATHER KNEW THIS WAS YOUR JOB...

...ASKING PEOPLE LIKE ME QUESTIONS LIKE THAT...

...WOULD HE BE PROUD OF *YOU?*

≥deet≥
deet≥
≥doot≥
≥daat
deet
deet
doot≥

YOU DONE WITH THE WARHORSE YET?

NOT QUITE. BUT HE'S DEFINITELY *NOT* GOING TO GIVE UP ANY-THING.

DOESN'T SURPRISE ME. WE'VE BEEN WATCHING HIM FOR YEARS AS PART OF THE BATMAN INVESTI-GATION.

GO AFTER THE SIDEKICK NEXT. MAYBE SHE KNOWS SOMETHING YOU CAN USE.

D.E.O.

J.H. Williams III: co-writer & artist   W. Haden Blackman: co-writer   Dave Stewart: colors   Todd Klein: letters

Rickey Purdin: asst. ed.    Harvey Richards: assoc. ed.    Michael Marts: editor    Batman created by Bob Kane

WE KNOW THAT BATWOMAN HAS A SIDEKICK. THE GIRL IN THAT GRAY UNIFORM WE KEEP CATCHING ON SECURITY CAMERAS? SHE'S A BLONDE.

COULD BE A WIG.

NO. WE COLLECTED BLONDE HAIRS FROM EACH OF THE SIDEKICK'S RECENT FIGHTS. THEY ALL MATCH. THEY ALL BELONG TO HER.

ONCE I REALIZED FLAMEBIRD'S ALSO A NATURAL BLONDE, AND ABOUT THE SAME SIZE AND AGE AS THE SIDEKICK, I COMPARED OUR SAMPLES TO HER HAIR.

ANOTHER PERFECT MATCH.

WE MAY NOT KNOW HER REAL NAME, BUT--

FLAMEBIRD IS THE BATWOMAN'S SIDEKICK.

I NEED TO CALL YOUR PARENTS, YOUR BOYFRIEND, ANYONE.

PLEASE, I DON'T WANT YOU TO DIE ALONE. IF YOU CAN HEAR ME, GIVE ME A NAME.

HUH... KATE...KATE KANE...

NOW THAT CAN'T BE A COINCIDENCE.

CHANGE HER DRESSINGS, ROLL HER OUT, AND DROP HER AT GOTHAM GENERAL.

SHE WON'T LAST THE NIGHT. NOT HERE, ANY-WAY.

Kate Kane survived a brutal kidnapping by terrorists that left her mother dead and her twin sister lost.

Following in her father's footsteps, she vowed to serve her country and attended West Point until she was expelled under "Don't Ask, Don't Tell."

Now she is many things: estranged daughter, grieving sister, proud lesbian, brave soldier, determined hero.

She is BATWOMAN.

BATWOMAN WILL RETURN in TO DROWN THE WORLD

This image of Batwoman, illustrated by J.H. Williams III,
was used for a DC Universe mural which is displayed in the
DC Entertainment offices.

Script excerpt from BATWOMAN #2 by W. Haden Blackman and J.H. Williams III.

## PAGE FOURTEEN/FIFTEEN (9 Panels)

The art here is more in style of the Batwoman look with shadows and textures.

Panel 5 is a central image across both pages, with the conversations happening in other panels surrounding it. So the main image of the entire scene runs through the middle of the spread from left to right. Panels 1, 2, and 3 are placed along the left side. Panel 5 is the largest panel on the page, in the middle of the spread, and silent, with two inset panels, these being panels 4 and 6. Panels 7, 8 and 9 run down the right side of the spread. So when Maggie's first line in panel 6 is read, it becomes two things: response to Chase, and a comment on the scene which this panel is inset, the full shot of all the dead.

Panel 5 is also the establishing shot of the location. Guttersnipe Gardens is basically a homeless encampment in the ruins of an old enclosed arboretum or giant greenhouse, perhaps something built for a World's Fair long ago. Now, it's just a rusting skeletal structure, with only a third of its windows still intact (but enough that it provides some shelter from the elements if you put up your tent or cardboard box in the right place). It's overgrown with leafless trees, mosses, and dead hanging plants. We can see it's still winter — there's snow on the ground, but only in patches and drifts (again to suggest that whatever remains of the windows and other parts of the structure offer some barest form of shelter).

Panel 1. Close-up of a puddle of blood in dirty looking snow, with spent bullet shell casings everywhere. We can see Chase's shoes as her feet barely touch the bloodied area of snow.

1-CHASE (OP):
Is there anywhere in Gotham that *doesn't* have bloodstains?

Panel 2. Semi-close on Chase, Bullock, and Maggie. We can't see what they're looking at yet, but we can see their expressions: Chase is annoyed; Bullock is his usual grumpy self; and Maggie is professional, keeping any emotions she might be feeling in check.

2-CHASE:
It's going to take days for my agents to collect all the shell casings.

3-BULLOCK:
At least no one got *snatched*, huh?

Panel 3. Chase, holding up a severed hand in an evidence bag, showing it to Bullock. Her body language and expression are a little aggressive, sarcastic — as if she's irritated with Bullock for not thinking things through a bit more.

4-CHASE:
Oh really? Well, *this* doesn't belong to any of the victims.

Panel 4. Inset into the giant panel 5. One of the DEO agents is kneeling next to a were-beast. We can't see the details of the were-beast here — just an arm or a tentacle. We can see the agent is taking tissue samples from the creature's appendage. The camera is low angled, looking up at Chase and Maggie as they look down at the agent. Chase is gesturing towards the corpse.

5-CHASE:
You know about these things?

Panel 5. Establishing shot of Guttersnipe Gardens (see above). In addition to the physical location described above, we can now see that there's a makeshift camp in the arboretum made up of tents, trash barrels for fires, and other signs of derelicts squatting. Some of the barrels have been knocked over, and there should be lots of evidence of a big fight having recently occurred here. The corpses of several were-beasts and Medusa thugs are strewn about. DEO agents are everywhere — they've clearly taken control of the crime scene. They are collecting clues, studying the bodies, taking photographs and notes. Chase, Maggie, and Bullock are in the center of the action. If we can see this from this angle Bullock is pissed, maybe arms crossed, defensive. Batwoman can be seen mixing into the details of the scene, hiding and spying.

NO COPY

Panel 6. Inset into the giant panel 4. The focus is on Maggie with Chase behind her.

6-MAGGIE:
In Gotham, there's the underworld and then there's the *underworld*. The were-beasts belong to the latter. They're an offshoot of the Religion of Crime led by a fanatic named Abbott.

7-CHASE:
I could have read that on-line.

Panel 7. Focus on Chase as she responds further to Maggie, Bullock in the Background with his arms crossed, clearly annoyed with the DEO stepping on their turf. In the shadowy structure we can see indications of Batwoman's cape as she spies.

8-CHASE:
I'll do you one better. Our snitches say this legion of freaks is at war with a rival gang.

Panel 8. Now Maggie is kneeling next to another body — one of the Medusa thugs, his stomach has been ripped open violently. We should be able to clearly see the Medusa symbol — a snake crest of some kind. Possibly Chase is nearby. Maggie is pointing/indicating towards the symbol.

9-MAGGIE:
Well, it *is* Gotham. So, yeah, that's probably accurate.

10-MAGGIE:
But these uniforms... *these* I don't recognize.

Panel 9. Close on Maggie, still kneeling next to the body, but looking grim, the weight of everything hitting her. Chase and Bullock dark in the background.

11-MAGGIE:
Just what we need... *another* new gang.

12-CHASE:
You think you know what happened here?

Black and white art by J.H. Williams III from BATWOMAN #2 pages 14-15 (above) and pages 16-17 (below).

Script excerpt from BATWOMAN #2 by W. Haden Blackman and J.H. Williams III.

**PAGE SIXTEEN/SEVENTEEN** (8 Panels)

The were-beast cultists here will be drawn and rendered like we've shown them before in Detective Comics (Batwoman: Elegy).

Most of this page is a big widescreen spread running across 2/3rds of the pages. It shows the fight between the were-beasts and Medusa's thugs, all happening at once, as if frozen in time. The Medusa thugs are mostly arranged in the middle and left side of the spread. Some were-beasts are crashing through windows on the right side of the spread, while another group is dropping into the center of the spread from above. Throughout the spread, Medusa thugs are gunning down were-beasts. In the center of the spread, the were-beasts are ripping into the thugs. We can also see two Medusa thugs, their backs largely to us, dragging a mysterious figure towards the bottom of the panel. The figure is a mentally ill homeless guy who has lost his left hand (chopped off), and who will eventually become the Hook. This man is actually Rush from all the way back in Detective Comics 854 page 1. But all of these details are somewhat unknown to us right now and we can't see much about him here, his back to us as Medusa things drag him towards us and about to go off panel... trailing blood from his wound. Finally, standing between the retreating Medusa thugs dragging the soon-to-be-Hook and the weres is a massive shadowy figure (Killer Croc, but we don't want the reader to know that because Chase and Maggie don't know yet — he should just be a huge shadow). His back is to us, and he's ripping apart one of the weres. He's surrounded by were corpses.

Maggie is walking through the scene like it's a big diorama, calling out specific moments in the fight (again, all seeming to happen at once in this panel, even though they might have occurred at different points in time during the actual fight). She's starting at the top left of the panel, making her way across towards the bottom right. Panels 1-5 call out what Maggie is saying and doing, but again these are just multiple images of Maggie moving through the bigger spread (if absolutely necessary, these can be insets).

The remaining space is taken up by a panel of Chase, oblivious to Batwoman hiding somewhere above her, and an inset showing Batwoman more clearly for the reader.

Panel 1. Maggie, starting at the top-left of the spread, looking around at the crime scene, which is now filled with images of the were-beasts and the Medusa thugs, as if drawn from Maggie's imagination.

(Again, note that the "panel" is really just Maggie's placement in the bigger spread — not a discrete panel on its own.)

1-MAGGIE:
Pretty routine ambush.

Panel 2. Maggie is kneeling near a pool of blood, only a few paces from where she started in "panel" 1. On the left side of the pool are armed Medusa thugs; on the right side, a group of were-beasts charging forward, some getting gunned down, others making it through and lashing out at the thugs. Members of both crews are already falling to the ground. We can see a trail of blood leading from the pool on the ground to the Medusa thugs dragging away their victim.

2-MAGGIE:
Unsubs attacked our missing victim here, but only managed to lop off his **hand** before Abbott's crew arrived.

NOTE: "Unsub" is jargon for "unidentified subject."

Panel 3. Maggie has moved a few paces towards the right of the panel, where the were-beasts are coming through the windows or over the makeshift rooftops. She's pointing towards the right, sort of directing our attention.

3-MAGGIE:
Based on the position of the bodies and the **debris** pattern, a first wave of weres came in from the east.

Panel 4. Maggie has moved further right, across the center of the spread, right where the were-beasts are dropping in from above, and in the middle of the conflict. She's looking up, pointing above.

4-MAGGIE:
But that was just a distraction. The second wave came in from **above**.

Panel 5. Maggie is standing right next to the Killer Croc silhouette stand-in. She's looking at the ground, where dead and dying weres have collected, looking at the evidence rather than the figure itself.

5-MAGGIE:
Something went wrong... Several weres look like they've been torn apart.

6-MAGGIE:
The unsubs had a **meta** with them. A big one.

Panel 6. Maggie has moved nearly to the bottom right now. She's pointing towards the blood trail left behind by the soon-to-be-Hook as he is being dragged away. It's imperative that we show his left hand missing from his body, dripping blood.

7-MAGGIE:
Unsure who won, but someone dragged the original victim away.

Panel 7. Low shot and close Chase, maybe hands on hips if we see that much of her. We're looking up at her, and can see past her, over her shoulder. A shadowy figure (Batwoman) lurks on top of one of the steel girders that forms the "roof" of the rotting arboretum, kneeling or standing and watching the scene unfold below.

Note: I may decide to combine 7 and 8 into a single image but use a panel box around Batwoman to isolate her from the shot of Chase.

8-CHASE:
Yeah, that's pretty much how we see it too.

Panel 8 (inset to panel 7). Zoom in on Batwoman atop the arboretum, hiding in the shadows, well out of view. She's looking down at the scene, though, and smiling.

9-BATWOMAN (whisper):
Nice work, babe.

The Hook character design by J.H. Williams III.

THE HOOK
CHARACTER DESIGN
2010

EVEN WITH A
HUNCHED OVER BACK
HE'S STILL ROUGHLY
6 ½ FEET TALL

SHORT LEGS
LONG ARMS

SORT OF A CROOKED FACE
WITH CLOSE TOGETHER INSET EYES
BAD TEETH WITH A GAP BETWEEN
TOP FRONT TEETH

BLEMISHED- PALE GREYISH WITH PINK BLOTCHES
FOR THE SKIN

NONE OF HIS CLOTHES FIT CORRECTLY

ALTHOUGH HE'S BRUTISH LOOKING
HE'S ACTUALLY QUITE INTELLIGENT

Design by J.H. Williams III for the Boathouse used in the first two story arcs of BATWOMAN.

Cover sketches by J.H. Williams III for BATWOMAN issues #0, 1, 4 and 5.